THE O ANTIPHONS
A STORYTELLER'S POINT OF VIEW

K. SEAN BUVALA

ILLUSTRATED BY MICHELLE BUVALA

WITH A PREFACE BY HARRIET COLE

SMALL-TOOTH-DOG PUBLISHING GROUP
TOLLESON, ARIZONA

O Antiphons: A Storyteller's Point of View

Published by:
Small-Tooth-Dog Publishing Group LLC
PO Box 392 Tolleson, AZ USA 85353

http://smalltoothdog.com

staff@smalltoothdog.com
Twitter: @smalltoothdog

©2019 by K. Sean Buvala.

Preface: Harriet Cole
Illustrations: Michelle M. Buvala

Second Edition

ISBN: 978-1-947408-00-5

All Rights Reserved. No part of this publication may be reproduced or redistributed in any form or by any means, including scanning, photocopying or otherwise without prior written permission of the copyright holder.

Please note: The editor and publisher have made every effort to be as accurate and complete as possible in the creation of this book. While all attempts have been made to verify information provided in this publication, the authors and publisher assume no responsibility for errors, omissions, or contrary interpretation of the subject matter herein. Any perceived slights of specific persons, peoples, or organizations are unintentional. This book is intended for the entertainment and enrichment of our readers.

DEDICATION

To those who understand that Liturgy is the crucible of Story and not the Story itself.

To those who know that ritual should serve people and not the other way around.

*The irony of Advent is that
we are called to be still, but not idle.*

O Antiphons: A Storyteller's Point of View

CONTENTS

Preface-: The O Antiphons and the Queen of the Otherworld 1

Night One- O Wisdom 9

Night Two- O Leader 11

Night Three- O Unexpected 13

Night Four-:O Key 14

Night Five- O DayBringer 19

Night Six- O King 25

Night Seven- O God With Us 27

Notes on the Stories 33

How To Use These Stories 37

About the Author 39

About the Artist 41

Contact 42

PREFACE— THE O ANTIPHONS AND THE QUEEN OF THE OTHERWORLD

Hanging out with Benedictines:

The *O Antiphons* and the Queen of the Otherworld

(Guest Preface by Harriet Cole)

My relationship with the season of Advent has always been … complicated.

I do not begrudge my neighbors their giant inflatable Santa Clauses and snowmen. My daily glimpses of red-and-white vinyl puddled at the base of a cactus entertain me. Yes, I do overdose on "The Little Drummer Boy" long before December 6. It could be worse. I used to have to play that stupid carol. And I will admit that I chuckle over neighborhoods so lit up that one street alone could turn back the darkness of the Winter Solstice.

Nevertheless, all these public festivities make me feel like a Christmas slacker. Hanging out with a small crowd of Benedictines has definitely improved my outlook on the Advent season.

Before I met these good people, I knew of only one kind of canon: the one in D Major.

What is a canon? Is a canon a cheerful and hospitable character wearing black robes or is a canon that which drives me crazy by making me play the same sequence of eight quarter notes fifty-eight times?

The short answer to this question: "yes." The word "canon" comes from the Greek *kanon*, which means "rule." A Benedictine Canon lives by the Rule of Saint Benedict, which is a set of instructions written in the sixth-century for monks living together in community. Pachelbel's Canon is the work of a sixteenth-century German composer who intentionally followed a specific set of musical rules.

Pachelbel followed his rules. The Benedictines follow their rules.

Aren't Benedictines monks like the fictional Brother Cadfael? Not all Benedictines. The word "monk" is derived from the Greek term for "solitary." This takes us back to the early Christians (male and female) who felt they could best serve their Lord by going into the desert to live by themselves. Over the centuries, the concept of a solitary life altered into the idea of living in enclosed communities. The word stayed the same.

The Benedictines I know belong to the contemporary Anglican Canon Communities of Saint Benedict. These men and women live in the secular world, with families and jobs while also living in vowed connection to the Rule of Saint Benedict. These are "my" canons and they gather regularly, either physically or spiritually, to pray the Daily Office.

As the name implies, the Daily Office is a pattern of prayers, readings, and psalms that occurs daily. It is – in short – a liturgy, a word defined by the dictionary as "a fixed set of ceremonies or words used in public worship."

As they work themselves through the yearly pattern of the Office, the canons eventually arrive – as do we all – in Advent where they find the *O Antiphons*. Generally speaking, an antiphon is a short sentence sung or recited before or after a psalm. The specific set known as the *O Antiphons* is sung during Vespers, the evening portion of the Daily Office, for seven days, ending December 23rd. This has been going on since at least the sixth century and possibly earlier.

But why? Why spend centuries saying almost the same thing over and over again seven evenings in a row? For that matter, why pray the Daily Office again and again? All that sounds kind of boring. Why don't these canons say their prayers in their own words, out of the fullness of their own hearts? Why don't we all speak directly from our hearts?

Because it's liturgy -- the words themselves are a ritual. On one level, rituals are repetitive and boring. And boring is good! Joseph Campbell, the mythologist most widely remembered by the advice in his book to "follow your bliss," said: "rituals are boring, they just wear you out, you know, and then you break through to something else." For the Benedictines (among others) the structure and rules of the Daily Office provide the focus necessary for breaking through to the creation of a sacred experience.

As a storyteller, I explore these same concepts of necessary structure and boundary. I often tell stories that are rooted in the oral narrative tradition. These folk and fairytales have very specific structures and boundaries. I also tell more or less self-revealing personal stories. In my life as a storyteller, these two genres, folktale and personal story, which seem to be very different, sometimes cross-fertilize.

Looking at the messy emotional truths of a personal story through the lens of a carefully chosen folktale helps focus the story I am trying to tell. I can craft stories about childhood challenges by turning to the structure and boundaries of a folktale like the Norwegian "Twelve Wild Ducks" in which a girl keeps silence to save her brothers from the evil spell that brought her into existence.

Sometimes I find one of my own stories lurking within the structure of a folktale. The Irish story "The Three Daughters of King O'Hara" from Jeremiah Curtin's *Myths and Folklore of Ireland*, came to life for me when I realized I had already lived this story. In this folktale, the king's third daughter seeks to rescue the man she loves from the clutches of the Queen of the Otherworld. Her quest includes following him into the Otherworld and using her small shreds of power to bargain with the queen. As is usual in European folktales, the girl has only three weapons, in this case a golden comb, a pair of golden scissors and a whistle made of gold. After she loses the comb and the scissors to the queen, she uses the whistle to ask the birds and beasts for advice. From them she learns how to kill the queen who – as is not uncommon in folktales like this – keeps her heart in an egg. Her ultimate success makes her man into the new King of the Otherworld.

When I teach storytelling at the community college level, I tell my first-time storytellers to work with the folktale they love. I fell in love with "The Three Daughters of King O'Hara" the first time I read it. I also tell my students that they cannot make a folktale their own until they hear what the story is saying. For all that I loved my story, I had trouble hearing its voice. I could see the tale as a variation on the Beauty and the Beast theme, but it did not speak to me the true and noble love that turns beast into a man. My heroine was no victim of her father's attempt to save himself. She misused his magic and ran off with a white dog! When the time came to rescue that white dog, there was nothing especially noble about her actions. She was stubborn. She kept running. She worked for the laundry maid and she bargained with the powerful queen.

Storytelling is a visual activity and I finally recognized my image of the Queen of the Otherworld. I knew that woman back in the 1970s. The folktale called forth memories of a time when I was young, foolish, and leading a chaotic life. This material was too confessional to craft into a personal story but the folktale provided the structure and boundaries for the emotional content of my story. When I tell "The Three Daughters of King O'Hara," I am telling my own story without saying a word about the 1970s. I spare my audience the confessional aspect of the story so that they can connect with the truth in the folktale.

The repetition of the liturgy serves the same purpose. I don't join my Benedictine friends as they chant the words of the *O Antiphons* during Advent, but I contemplate those words:

O Wisdom ... come and teach us the way of prudence.

O Lord and Ruler of the house of Israel ... come and redeem us with outstretched arms.

O Root of Jesse ...come to deliver us, and tarry not.

O Key of David ... come and lead forth the captive who sits

in the shadows from his prison.

O Dawn of the East … come and enlighten those who sit in darkness and in the shadow of death.

O King of the Gentiles … come and deliver mankind, whom you formed out of the dust of the earth.

O Emmanuel, God with us … come and save us.

For me, these words keep chaos at bay in a way the fullness of my heart cannot. My heart gets tangled up with inflatable plastic snowmen, too many decorations, and my self-judgments. The *O Antiphons* help me remember that the "Ad" in "Advent" is not the "Ad" in "Advertising."

*The Kingdom of God is at hand.
Here and now. Still someday.*

NIGHT ONE- O WISDOM

"O Wisdom, you come forth from the mouth of the Most High. You fill the universe and hold all things together in a strong yet gentle manner. O come to teach us the way of truth."

Story: A young boy was making his way home after a long day of working as the apprentice to a craftsman. His day had been so long and tiring, that he could barely keep his eyes open. He thought he might lie down for just a few moments and so found a place in the grass to rest.

When he fell asleep, Lady Fortune looked down upon him. She saw that he had actually made his bed at the very edge of a deep hole in the ground. At that moment, she flew down to him and nudged him awake.

She said, "Rise, young man, and be on your way. For surely, if you had fallen into the hole, I would be the one blamed. Rather, next time, look carefully where you step and lay your head."

-Adapted from an Aesop tale

K. Sean Buvala

NIGHT TWO- O LEADER

"O Leader of the House of Israel! Come to us! Rescue us with your mighty power."

Story: Once there was a group of worker bees who built a hive full of honeycomb inside a hollow tree. Not long after that, a party of drone bees flew past and saw the honey. They forcibly ejected the worker bees from the tree, proclaiming that they, the drones, now owned the honey.

Obviously, the workers were upset with this. They demanded that the drones leave them alone. The drones refused. The two parties then decided that they would ask the Lord Wasp to settle the dispute.

Upon reaching the nest of the Wasp, they all began to buzz and chatter at once, creating a great deal of noise, trying to explain why each party should have ownership of the honey.

The Lord Wasp said, "You make such a noise and I cannot tell your winged groups apart. I say this: each party should go into sections of my tree and make honeycomb. I will then decide which of your groups is most talented. I will award your disputed tree to the winners."

The worker bees agreed with the plan immediately. The drones did not, as they knew that they could not make honey themselves. They protested to the Lord Wasp as he had proposed an impossible task.

"Well then." he wisely replied, "I award the disputed honeycomb to the worker bees as it seems they are the only ones who are both eager and capable to make such a fine home and meal."

–Adapted from an Aesop tale

NIGHT THREE- O UNEXPECTED

"O Root of Jesse, you stand among the nations who sing your praise. Come and deliver us."

Story: The animals decided that they needed a king. And among all the animals, it was considered that the birds were the wisest and trustworthy, for in the time of the start of the world, they spoke a language that all creatures could understand. From the birds, a king would be chosen.

A contest was arranged. Whichever bird could fly the highest would be king. On the day of the contest, all the birds assembled and in one great show of feather and strength, they all rose to take flight.

Higher and higher they flew, but one by one, the birds would drop out of the race with the smallest of the birds among the first to quit the race. The distance to the top of the sky was too far; their small wings could not take the work of so much flight.

At last, the eagle alone remained flying higher and higher. When he saw that he was the last remaining contestant, he cried out in joy and began his descent. At the very moment, the wren, who had hidden in the feathers of the eagle, flew away from the eagle. The wren, having been carried by the eagle, could now fly higher until it appeared that he flew high enough to touch the edges of heaven.

The animals and birds then named the wren as king, joyful that the small bird had shown great ingenuity.

To this day, the wren is called the King of Birds.

-Adapted from Grimm and Aesop tales.

NIGHT FOUR- O KEY

"O Key of David. Come set us free of our chains and darkness. Free us, bring us home."

Story: There once was a Princess, young into her adulthood, who had not spoken a word since she was 12 years old. Over the many years, the king had called upon every doctor and priest to try to make his daughter better. Yet, still, she spoke not a word.

From the castle, word was sent out far and wide. The king promised that the man who could heal his daughter and give her voice would then have her hand in marriage.

For months, many men came to apply their earnest efforts to cure the princess. Yet, no one could cure her.

Finally, one day, a young man named William came to the kingdom. When it was his turn to attempt to cure the princess, he spoke not a word to her. Rather, as she looked on, William spoke to the Princess' little dog.

"Little dog," William began, "I want to tell you a story from my life. Recently, some fellow artisans and I set out on a long journey. One night, after we made camp and the light was fading, my friend the woodsman cut down a lovely tree, creating a perfect log that stood in the center of our camp.

Then, I, a sculptor, used my tools to carve the log into the shape and form of a pretty woman. The third among us, a tailor, created an exquisite dress to place upon the wooden lady. Afterward, we all slept very soundly. However, when we awoke, the wooden lady had transformed into a real woman. Of course, we three artisans, myself included, began to argue about to whom she belonged. I ask you, little dog, to whom did our lady belong? Tell me if you can."

The small dog simply cocked his head and wagged his tail. However, from across the room, the Princess cleared her throat. She began to speak, much to the astonishment and awe of all assembled.

"I suppose, Master Carver, that the woman would 'belong' to whomever she chose. She alone would make the choice to marry and to whom she would marry. You agree, do you not?"

William looked at the Princess. He nodded.

I probably don't need to tell you how the Princess did decide to marry. You may be assured that it was she that chose William after years of courtship.

- Adapted from English and Slavic Tales, some attributed to A.H. Wratislaw.

"God is subtle, but he is not malicious."
-A. Einstein

NIGHT FIVE- O DAYBRINGER

"Come, O Day-Bringer. Come, Light, and rescue those in shadow and darkness."

Story: There was a time when all of the animals could speak.

And, at that time, there were ten suns in the sky. So many suns filling the sky. As you can imagine, it was hot all the time. There was no relief. It was bright and searing. The animals were unhappy.

The animals began to beg the suns for relief. They said, "Suns, would you please take turns in the sky? We cannot survive in all of this heat and light. Would you please, we beg you, take turns in the sky?"

But the suns laughed. "No! We are brothers and we will share the sky together at any time we like. You will have to put up with ten of us in the sky."

And so it was for a very long time.

But one day, appearing in the village of the animals was an animal no one had ever seen before. It was a small, white bird. We would know it now as a dove. The dove said to the animals, "I understand that you have a problem with the suns in the sky."

"Yes, yes we do," replied the animals.

The dove said, "Well if you would like, I will ask the suns to leave. And, if they will not leave, I will make them leave."

The animals readily agreed to the plan. They took the dove to the place where the suns lived, next to a cave near a flowing river. The dove looked up at the suns and she said, "Suns, the animals have asked you to leave and to only have one of you in the sky at a time. Will you not honor their request?"

The suns laughed. They refused. They still said no.

"Very well, as you wish," said the dove. "Then, I will begin my dance." The dove began to dance so beautifully in a way that no one, no animal, nothing on earth had ever seen. They had never known anything so beautiful. It was flawless and mesmerizing. The more she danced, the more interested the suns became. They drew closer and closer to the dove in order to see her dance.

When each of them got close enough to the dove, she would suddenly reach up high, pull a sun from the sky and cast him into the river where he was extinguished and died.

She moved so quickly, so unexpectedly. She reached into the sky and pulled down another sun, casting it into the river where its light and heat would be put out. She reached into the sky, pulled down a sun! Over and over again, she repeated the process, sending each sun to their death until only one sun remained.

The last sun saw what had happened to his brothers and he was afraid. He decided that such a fate would not befall him! He ran deep into the cave, hiding very far back in the cave.

When he disappeared, the light and warmth of the world vanished. And with that, the dove vanished as well.

Now, the animals were cold. It was dark in the world. They were afraid.

They looked into the cave and they called out, "Sun! Come back out. Come back out, please. We need you."

However, the sun refused.

After some time, the rooster came upon an idea. He said, "Let me ask. I will try."

He walked to the cave. He looked deep into the cavern and said playfully, "Are you going to come out or what are you going to do?"

"No! I am not coming out. I have seen what terror awaits me," said the sun.

"Well," laughed the rooster, "I just think it is kind of funny that you are in there."

The rooster began to laugh louder. "Co-co-co! Doo-dodo-doo! Doodle doodle doodle!"

As he laughed, he would take a step back from the cave and then laugh a little more. He moved further and further back from the cave.

At this point, the sun was wondering why the rooster would laugh so loud. He began to follow the rooster out of the cave. With each back step of the rooster, the sun grew closer to the mouth of the cave.

"Coco doodle do!" The rooster kept laughing!

Then, even this last sun began to laugh. He moved closer to the mouth of the cave when, in a fit of laughter with the rooster, he slipped from the mouth of the cave. He laughed so hard that he launched himself into the sky!

The rooster had one heartier laugh. "Coco Doodle Do!"

To this day, it is the rooster that is calling out a rising sun.

-Created by Sean for his collection "Calling Out a Rising Sun: Stories for Teenage Guys." callingoutarisingsun.com

Emmanuel is here and yet still comes.

NIGHT SIX- O KING

"Come, O Great King! Bless us the creatures you have formed from the earth."

Story: The Sun and the Wind were having a disagreement about who among them was the greater.

It was the wind trumpeting on about his greatness. The Sun, in his wisdom, was mostly nodding in agreement but maintained it was he that was the more powerful of the two.

"I wish to argue no longer," said the Wind. "I challenge you to a test to see who is greater."

"I agree," calmly stated the Sun.

The Wind looked to the earth and said, "See. There is a man below who is dressed in garments. Whichever of us can cause him to remove the outer garment surely is the greater, for only we can control such creatures of the earth."

"Proceed as you will," replied the Sun.

The Wind began to blow across the man, stirring up dirt and cloud, blowing hard at the human walking below. No matter how hard he tried, the man would not remove the garment. Indeed, the fellow, against the Wind's now chill embrace, wrapped the garment around himself even tighter.

"It is of no use to try," said the Wind when he could no longer bluster at the man.

"No, it is my turn," the Sun said as he turned his gaze upon the person walking below. Rather than gust, upset, or harass the man, the Sun simply let his gaze shine upon the man. As the clouds from the previous attempt vanished, the man looked up at the sky. As the air around him grew warmer and more comfortable in the simple gaze of the sun, the man removed his outer garment and carried on his way.

At the point, the Wind did concede that the gentle Sun was indeed the greater of the two.

-Adapted from an Aesop table.

NIGHT SEVEN— O GOD WITH US

"O Come, Emmanuel!"

Story: "Ohhhhhh!" she said, more loudly than she intended but as loudly as she thought it. It was a long, guttural and frustrated "Ohhhhh!" as she banged on that vending machine that had taken, or stolen, her last dollar.

That outburst might have gotten attention anywhere else, but would not usually in an airport. For those traveling, sitting in the chairs, waiting for the gates to open, only the very new would even bother to lower their newspapers, tablets, and smart-phones.

But her distinct "ohhhhh," merely the start of a truncated swear, made them all look up. They only looked up for a moment, you understand. "If she'd just shut up those screaming kids," was the thought of most of them.

Those kids were all under five and crying, the youngest in a diaper that clearly needed attention.

And she banged on that vending machine one more time, the one that took her last sad dollar. She was on the run, leaving the scene, answering the "why doesn't she just leave him" question for all to see. Her last hope was that bottle of water stuck in the stupid machine, one single dollar away.

She needed that water. Who would want to make formula out of the sludge that came from the taps in this airport?

Suddenly he appeared, standing right there at the machine. He looked at the woman and said, "Hey, you got change for a five?"

She looked at him, bewildered. She thought to herself, "Are you the only one who is not watching my meltdown right here in the middle of the airport?"

"No, I don't have change. This fouled-up machine ate the last of my money."

"Oh! Wait wait wait. I do have change," he said as he reached into his coat pocket. There it was: a small little stack of vending-machine-perfect one-dollar bills.

He slid off one of those perfect bills and stuck it in the machine. Ffffpppt. It went in perfectly. Not ffffpppt in and then spat out, but ffffpppt right in and stayed in the machine.

And then, to her dismay, he punched in the vending machine numbers she feared he would use….G6…G you gotta be kidding me 6. He was buying the bottle of water. That bottle was the last one in the machine and her kid was thirsty.

She glanced his way, her last ounce of courage was bundling up in her heart. She plastered on a fresh face, looked at him and flirted. "You know, that's the last bottle of water in this whole smelly place. It is the only one left to make formula with. What do I have to do to get it from you, honey?"

And he said, playfully, "You thought you'd just pretty-eyes it away from me, huh?"

"Whatever works, Mister," she replied.

"How come your husband won't get you a bottle of water, you with all those yelling babies?"

Her mind flashed full of anger. Resentment and fear, fresh from the reasons for her running in the first place, filled her tired heart.

"It's none of your business," she spat out at him.

"No, but this bottle of water is my business. I bought it for you. Here, take it." He held out the bottle to her.

Too tired to figure out the riddle of this stranger with the perfect one-dollar bills, she grabbed the water bottle, mumbled "thank you," and began to gather up her kids.

"Wait, hold on a second," he said as he reached down into his traveling bag. As he dug around, he said to her, "Where ya' going?"

"Dodge City, Kansas. My momma lives there and she will

help me out while I figure out all this stuff with my husband..and…why am I telling you this?"

He pulled his hands out of his bag, In his right hand, he held three bottles of water by the caps. In his left hand was a business card.

Thrusting his left hand forward, he said, "Take these bottles. These are all for you."

"I can't pay for those," she said.

"Did I ask you to pay for them? You owe me nothing in exchange. I have plenty for myself."

"Well, umm, thanks, then." She stuffed the bottles into her baby's bag.

"And," he said, as he pointed to something on the back of the business card, "when you get to Dodge City, Kansas, you call the 'Everlast Community Outreach Center' there. You tell them that Jesse sent you. The number is here on the card. You call them, you let them help you and get some counseling, too."

"I don't need no counseling from…" she spat back, but he cut her off.

"You really must call them and let them help you out." And there was an authority of a person who understood.

"Jesse who?" she asked.

"Look at the card," was his reply.

His name on the card was "Jesse." No last name but the line underneath said "Everlast Water Company: President." The logo on his card was the same as the one on the bottles of water.

"Now," he said, "will you call them when you land in Dodge City?"

"Yes, I will."

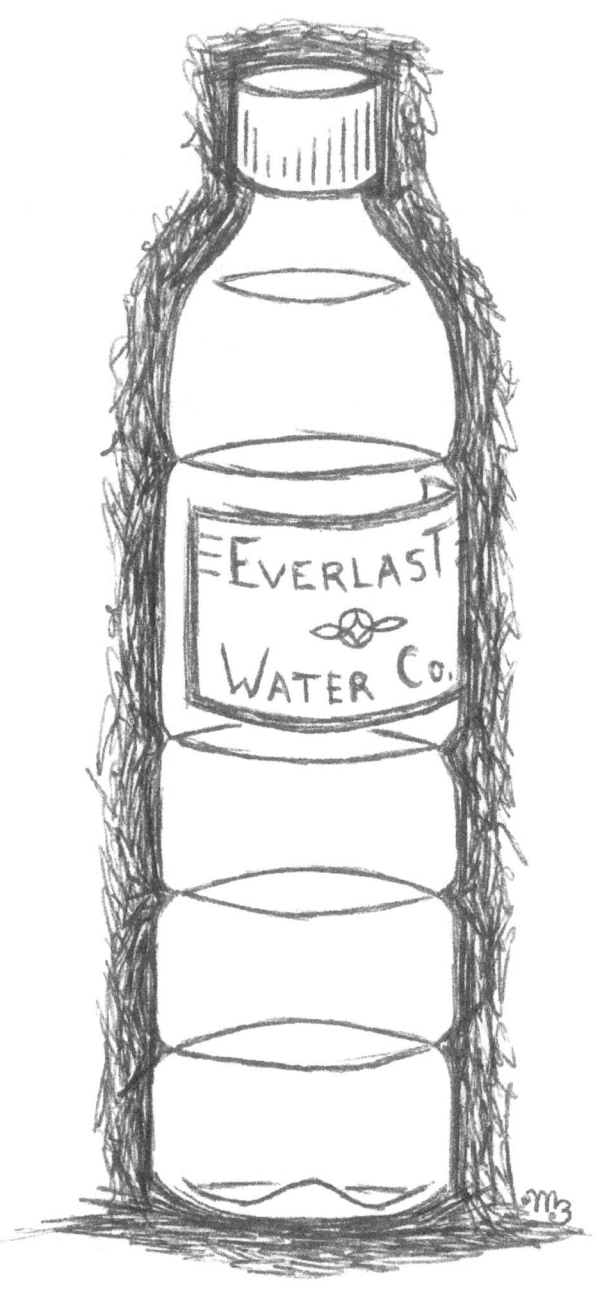

She gathered up her stuff, secured the babies in the stroller, and took the eldest child by the hand. She surely left nothing at all behind.

She started to make her way down the terminal to her gate. She turned around to ask him one more question, but he was nowhere to be found.

When she got to Dodge City, there was a story to be told about the bizarre man in the airport. Her mother thought it was good news.

NOTES ON THE STORIES

These notes are a bit cryptic, perhaps, if you are not familiar with Christian theology or Scripture. I automatically think in narrative. These are neither prose nor prosaic; they are just my thoughts from my personal reflection on these stories and the Antiphons. If I confuse you too much, ask around or Email me.

One: "The Boy at the Well." The Spirit moves as she will. Wisdom shows as the babe in the manger, the teacher on the hill, the one who validated the importance of the "doubt" that Thomas reportedly showed. Wisdom whispers at the edge of danger. Frankly, Wisdom has probably been warning us all along, but we are too busy to notice. It's odd to call out to a teacher who never really leaves us. In my youth-group leader years, I used to tell the kids to "put yourselves in the presence of God" to quiet them for prayer circles. As I got older in years and wiser in ministry, I understood better. We can't put ourselves in the presence of God as we are already and always in it at the edge of the well and everywhere. I eventually learned to remind them that they were (we are) always in the presence of God.

Two: "The Battle of the Bees." The Incarnation is incarnate in us. Great powers have stolen the work (and stories) of the poor throughout history. This injustice is universal and seems to be incorporated into our being as humans. Dystopian youth-literature makes it the underpinning of nearly every series; look to *The Hunger Games*, *The Giver* and the like. Leaders, divine and more, see that the work is from the worker. Rescue is in Wisdom, or was that on the first night?

Three: "The Eagle and the Wren." Speaking of dystopian-future youth novels, the "one who rises from oppression" is nearly biblical, isn't it? The great eagle is, at first, the obvious winner. But then, the wren flies forth from within the wings of the eagle. Some people who hear me tell this story get ruffled about the wren's "cheating." Didn't God cheat when the Savior came from Nazareth? "Really, God? That is the best you can do: pulling a Savior from a nether city of the Roman empire?" Cheater. Leaders can make great things happen against impossible odds, against apparent winners, or was that the second night?

Four: "The Princess and the Carver." Much like night one, I am not so sure that God wants us to wait to be set free. We have a voice, we should use it. We have the ability to think, to create, to challenge. We should use it? For me, most of what Emmanuel does is sending down more questions. The trick, however, is that God asks the right question. Have you answered the right question lately? The Savior knows that from apparent nothing can come answers, or was that the third night?

Five: "Calling Out a Rising Sun." Years ago, I created this story, one that is similar to stories across many cultures, for a potential program on addiction recovery using the arts such as storytelling and music. If there is ever shadow and darkness, it is when something has itself tentacled around your desire, whether that is, among other things, alcohol, rage, drugs, or sex. For some, the Savior is supposed to be the dove, right? That is the religious thing at least. Rather, the dance is deceit, It extinguishes the whole instead of the part. Then, it vanishes, leaving desecration and cold. The rooster, like the wren of night three or Katniss of *Hunger Games* or Jesus of Nazareth, is the one who calls out the sun, rescues from darkness. But, still, in the end, the sun must come from the cave. Maybe someone is asking you if you are going to leave your own cave, or was that back on night four?

Six: "The Sun and the Wind." One of the most well-known Aesop tales slipped its way into my book. It's pretty simple: the Savior is one who knows; who acts not to draw attention to the Savior but to the saved, the redeemed. Sometimes the right question is not a question, but a presence and a calling out, or was that night five?

Seven: "The Woman at the Vending Machine." My most complicated story I've created for "church." It was originally for the Lenten season, specifically a variant on the "Samaritan Woman at the Well." I've twisted it here slightly and cleaned up the language. It is part of my "Bible Stories I Can't Tell at Church" series. As I reread it, I was reminded: Christmas has little real meaning without Easter. To reduce Christmas to celebrating Baby Jesus is to deny the challenging, provoking Wren of Nazareth who asked the right questions, gently loved when needed, warned when needed, gave hope when needed and asked a woman that everyone else avoided for a drink from her very own water bottle. Of course, he knew that she didn't have change; none of us do. Change comes from the Emmanuel we meet from all seven nights of the *O Antiphons*.

HOW TO USE THESE STORIES

In a few words, my answer is: I don't know. This has been a personal spirituality project of mine for many years, even after I was done being employed in various ministries across the United States. I have had other stories speak to me for each of the nights, but these were the ones that stuck with me the most when I started to write this project down way back in 2015.

So, how will you use these stories, these writings? Maybe:

:: Read a story for each day during the O Antiphons. Let it sink in. Roll it about in your head. It might or might not fit for you. Or.

:: Use them as part of an already existing prayer-group. Take turns reading the story out loud each night. Better, ask seven people to each learn one story to tell on its night, knowing it well enough to put the book down and tell it in their own voice and in their words, not mine. Getting the words right for these stories is not important. Telling them is important. Or.

:: Make a day-long Advent retreat for your church or groups within your church, using these stories for seven sessions. Tell the stories, talk about them. Agree with them or wonder what the heck I was thinking. Sing. Pray. Eat. Have lots of eating as it's the most liturgical thing you can do outside of Liturgy. If you need bulk copies of books for your group, contact me. I can arrange a decent price for you. Don't make your own copies of this book "just this once" or ever. Our workers are worthy of their wage. Please contact me first before you copy. Or.

:: Invite me to come to tell these stories (or any of hundreds) for your small-group, your retreat, your workshop, your parish's multi-night retreat, your drum circle, your wedding, your funeral. Contact me, and we will work something out. Use the contact form at www.seantells.com/contact. Thanks.

Dear reader, in whatever you decide, I wish you Pax Tecum or Blessed Be,

-Sean

ABOUT THE AUTHOR

Sean Buvala

Sean Buvala has been engaged with storytelling and communication since 1986. He started his work by accidentally using active storytelling to convert a classroom of slightly (but comically) homicidal 8th-grade teenagers in a parochial school from angry kids to storytelling practitioners themselves. From then on, both the kids and Sean were sold on the strong influence of a great story.

An author, publisher, speaker, workshop leader and performance artist, Sean describes the collection of stories in his head as "life and legend" representing the mix of tales from his experiences, myth, and legend from many cultures, sacred stories and observations of shared life events. He is the executive director of *Storyteller.net* and the publisher at *The Small-Tooth-Dog Publishing Group LLC*.

As far as "what religion are you anyway," he is a Catholic in the Old-Catholic denomination (they are progressive) and has been on staff for both Roman-Catholic and Protestant churches and publishers.

Father of four young adults and husband to one wife, he lives in the desert southwest of the Phoenix, Arizona area but travels nationally. Find more at seantells.com

Harriet Cole (Preface)

It seems oddly fitting that Harriet Cole first heard the call to tell stories while she was sitting in a pew not listening to the sermon. Since that time, she has blended her storytelling and her approach to spiritual life with varying degrees of success – sometimes there is a more secular story, sometimes more sacred telling. As the coordinator of the Intergenerational Storytellers at Saint Augustine's Episcopal Parish, she coaches youth tellers, offers storytelling workshops to all ages, and coordinates the Scripture as oral stories as part of the Easter Vigil.

As a storyteller, she has performed her Norse programs at the Musical Instrument Museum and for local Scandinavian groups. She has also told stories at the South Mountain Environmental Education Center and with the Arizona Republic AZ Storytellers Project. She has also performed and presented a workshop at the National Storytelling Network Conference. Learn more about Harriet's storytelling activities (including her work as an Adjunct Instructor at the South Mountain Community College Storytelling Institute) on her website: www.harrietcolestoryteller.com

ABOUT THE ARTIST

About the Art

For this book, Michelle interpreted each story via simple sketch and Scribble art, appropriate for the season of Advent. Each picture is hand-drawn in pen and ink.

About the Artist

Some people are born with a great gift to create with their hands. Michelle Buvala is one of those people. Whether she's helping children create fun, wearable art or growing fresh vegetables in her garden, her family and friends are amazed by her creativity and ability to create something good from the simplest components.

In her life, she has worked in many places, from the excitement of the toy store to the daily challenges of the classroom. She's an avid desert gardener and a founder of the local community garden in her city.

Michelle holds a degree in Elementary Education from the Arizona State University. She is the founder of The Mesquite Tree Studio in Avondale, Arizona. Her first illustrated children's book is *Apples for the Princess* and is available on Amazon, too.

CONTACT

Website:

http://oantiphons.com

Sean Buvala is happy to hear from you. Try:

Twitter: @storyteller
Personal Newsletter: seantells.com/wednesday
Facebook: facebook.com/seanbuvala
Instagram: instagram.com/seantells
Website: seantells.com
Email: seantells@gmail.com

Sean, Michelle, and Harriet have many of books, published via The Small-Tooth-Dog Publishing Group. smalltoothdog.com.

www.ingramcontent.com/pod-product-compliance
Lightning Source LLC
Chambersburg PA
CBHW061303040426
42444CB00010B/2490